SOLVING SCIENCE MYSTERIES

W9-BHS-375

Why Do Airplanes Fly?

All About Flight

Rob Moore

PowerKiDS press.

New York

Published in 2010 by The Rosen Publishing Group, Inc.
29 East 21st Street, New York, NY 10010

Produced and designed by Denise Ryan & Associates
Editor: Helen Moore and Edwina Hamilton
Designer: Anita Adams
Photographer: Lyz Turner-Clark
U.S. Editor: Joanne Randolph

Photo Credits: p. 4 top: © Photographer: Frans Sluijs | Agency: Dreamstime.com; p. 6 top: Steve Smith and World of Stock; p. 6 middle left: Ivan Cholakov; p. 6 middle right: © Photographer: Warren Parsons | Agency: Dreamstime.com; p. 6 bottom: Lenny Flank; p. 7 top: © Photographer: Igor Zhorov | Agency: Dreamstime.com; p. 7 bottom: © Photographer: Paul Maguire | Agency: Dreamstime.com; p. 8 top: © Photographer: Alle | Agency: Dreamstime.com; p. 8 bottom: Ken Babione; p. 9 top: © Photographer: Brad Thompson | Agency: Dreamstime.com; p. 9 second from top: Ronen; p. 9 third from top: Sonja Foos; p. 9 bottom: © Photographer: Craig Joiner | Agency: Dreamstime.com; p. 10: NASA; pp. 11, 16 top: Photolibrary; p. 13 top left: Getty Images; p. 13 top right: Photolibrary; 13 bottom: Adrian Pingstone; p. 14 top left: © Photographer: Yemeky | Agency: Dreamstime.com; p. 14 top right: © Photographer: Dr. Pramod Bansode | Agency: Dreamstime.com; p. 14 bottom: © Photographer: Jp Mice | Agency: Dreamstime.com; p. 15 top: © Photographer: Sean Nel | Agency: Dreamstime.com; p. 15 middle: AAP Images; p. 18 top © Science Photo Library, p. 18 bottom © Photo by Michael Ochs Archives|Getty Images; p. 19 top: National Museum of American History, Smithsonian Institution; p. 22 left © www.istockphoto.com/Andrew Rich.

Library of Congress Cataloging-in-Publication Data

Moore, Rob.
  Why do airplanes fly? : all about flight / Rob Moore.
      p. cm. — (Solving science mysteries)
  Includes index.
  ISBN 978-1-61531-890-2 (lib. bdg.) — ISBN 978-1-61531-912-1 (pbk.) —
ISBN 978-1-61531-923-7 (6-pack)
  1. Flight—Miscellanea—Juvenile literature. 2. Aerodynamics—Miscellanea—Juvenile literature. I. Title.
  TL547.M66 2010
  629.132'3—dc22

                                 2009031078

Manufactured in the United States of America

CPSIA Compliance Information: Batch #WW10PK: For Further Information contact Rosen Publishing, New York, New York at 1-800-237-9932

Contents

Questions About Flight

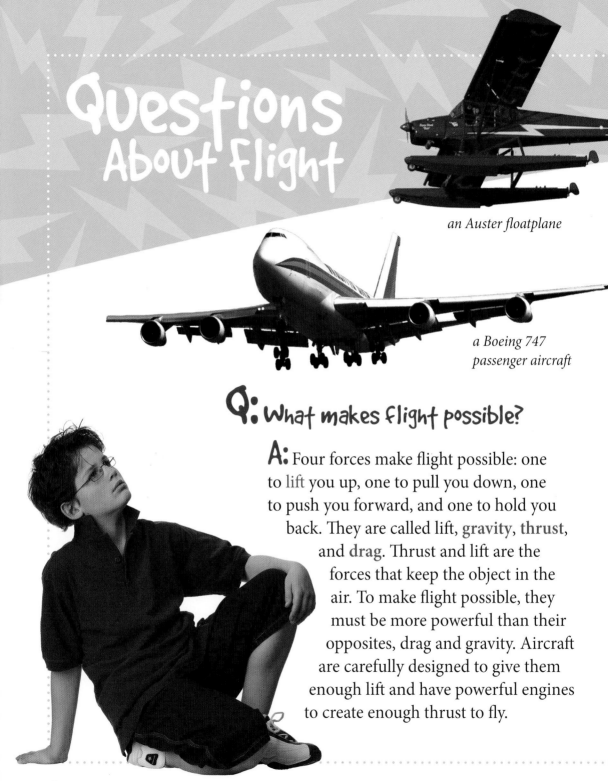

an Auster floatplane

a Boeing 747 passenger aircraft

Q: What makes flight possible?

A: Four forces make flight possible: one to lift you up, one to pull you down, one to push you forward, and one to hold you back. They are called lift, **gravity**, **thrust**, and **drag**. Thrust and lift are the forces that keep the object in the air. To make flight possible, they must be more powerful than their opposites, drag and gravity. Aircraft are carefully designed to give them enough lift and have powerful engines to create enough thrust to fly.

Q: Who flew the first aircraft?

A: The Wright brothers flew the first successful flying machine in 1903. One engine attached to the frame turned **propellers** and created enough power to keep the aircraft moving forward. This provided essential lift from air rushing under and over the wings to keep it airborne.

This is the 1903 Wright Flyer at the Smithsonian National Air and Space Museum in Washington, D.C.

Q: How does a jet engine work?

A: Jet engines work just like releasing an inflated balloon and having the escaping air propel the balloon in the opposite direction. First, they suck air in at the front with a fan. The air is then **compressed** and sprayed with fuel. An electric spark lights the mixture. The burning gases expand and blast out through a nozzle at the back of the engine. As the jets of gas shoot backward, the engine and the aircraft are thrust forward.

This is how air flows through a jet engine.

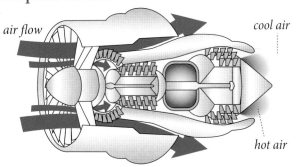

air flow

cool air

hot air

5

Q: How do aircraft wings work?

A: An aircraft's wing area must be large enough to give enough lift for it to be able to fly. The shape of the aircraft's wings makes the air on top of the wings move faster than the air below them. The air below the wings is **denser** so it pushes the wings from below, giving the aircraft lift. The faster an aircraft can travel the less wing area is needed, so jet fighters often have smaller wings compared to those of cargo aircraft.

above aircraft
fast moving air
lower pressure than below the aircraft

below aircraft
dense air
air pushing the wings

an F16 Falcon at an air show in 2006

a C17 Globemaster III —a cartgo aircraft

an F16 Falcon —a jet fighter

an F15 Eagle—a jet fighter

Cargo aircraft have large wings to give them lift. Jet fighters have smaller wings because they move through the air very quickly.

Q: How do gliders stay up in the air?

A: Gliders have no thrust so they must be towed or launched into the sky to give them **momentum**. Their long, slender wings give great lift but they need "thermals" to sustain their flight. Thermals are patches of air that rise because they are warmer than the surrounding air. A glider needs to use the lift of this warmer air to gain height.

Flying High

Birds and insects fly by using their wings to lift off the ground and to support their weight on currents of air. Although humans have never had wings, they have always wanted to fly. Scientists and inventors looked for ways to make artificial wings for hundreds of years. The Italian artist and inventor Leonardo da Vinci drew designs for flying machines in the early 1500s.

Questions About Bumblebees and Kites

Q: Why can a bumblebee fly?

A: People used to believe that bumblebees should not be able to fly because their wings are too flat and small and their bodies are too round and heavy. However, the bumblebee uses its wings more like a helicopter than an airplane. They rotate their wings very quickly, at about 200 beats a second. A bumblebee flies forward by tipping its wings down at the front. This action turns lift into thrust.

Q: Why can kites fly?

A: Kites fly using the force of lift. The kite is held by its line at an angle to the wind, so that it is lifted rather than pushed. Lift works in an upward direction, opposing the pull of gravity on the kite. Some kites have a tail, which acts like an anchor and provides **stability**. The tail causes drag, which holds the bottom of the kite down and steady. If the line is released, the kite becomes a glider and gradually descends to Earth because it has no thrust.

9

Questions About High Flight

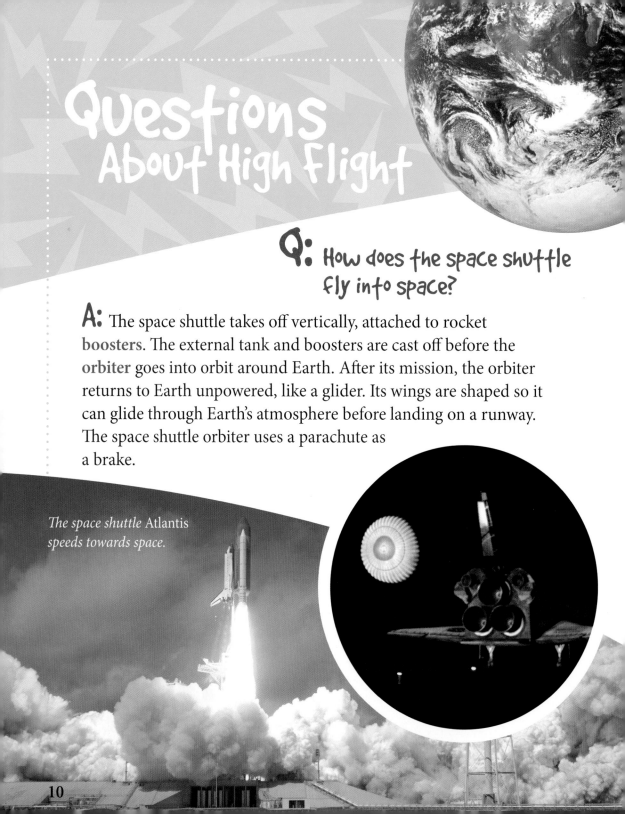

Q: How does the space shuttle fly into space?

A: The space shuttle takes off vertically, attached to rocket **boosters**. The external tank and boosters are cast off before the **orbiter** goes into orbit around Earth. After its mission, the orbiter returns to Earth unpowered, like a glider. Its wings are shaped so it can glide through Earth's atmosphere before landing on a runway. The space shuttle orbiter uses a parachute as a brake.

The space shuttle Atlantis *speeds towards space.*

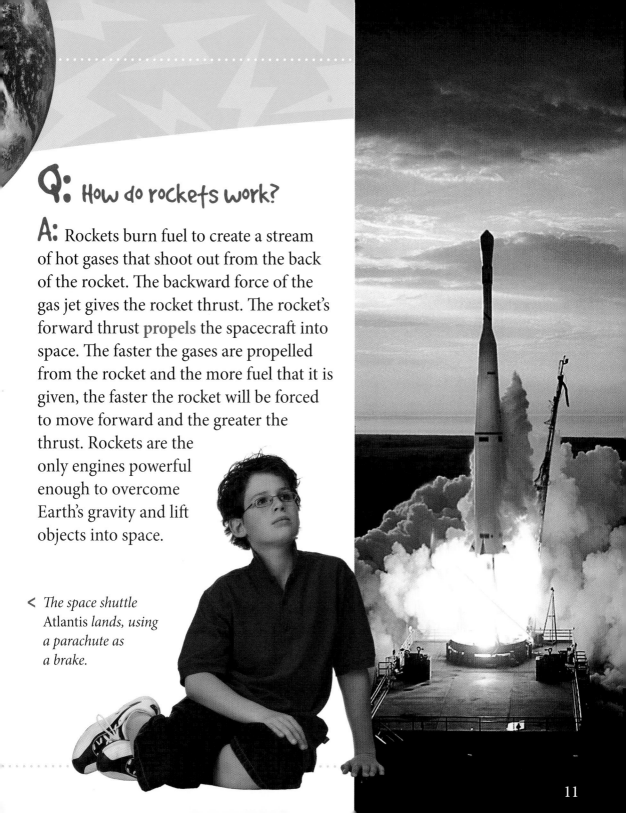

Q: How do rockets work?

A: Rockets burn fuel to create a stream of hot gases that shoot out from the back of the rocket. The backward force of the gas jet gives the rocket thrust. The rocket's forward thrust **propels** the spacecraft into space. The faster the gases are propelled from the rocket and the more fuel that it is given, the faster the rocket will be forced to move forward and the greater the thrust. Rockets are the only engines powerful enough to overcome Earth's gravity and lift objects into space.

< *The space shuttle Atlantis lands, using a parachute as a brake.*

It's a Fact

> Dirigibles

Dirigibles were used for passenger transport in the 1920s and 1930s, but after the disastrous explosion of the German Hindenburg in New Jersey in 1937, they lost favor with passengers.

> Airships

Simple **airships** were used for military observation as early as the eighteenth century. In World War II airships were used as a guard against enemy aircraft. Cables were trailed beneath the floating airships, blocking the path of aircraft.

> Two in One

The Harrier jump jet can land and take off vertically like a helicopter but flies like a jet. It has movable jet nozzles that can be changed to allow the aircraft to take off vertically but to fly horizontally.

This is the Hindenburg, *immediately after catching fire.*

> Jet Set

The de Havilland Comet was the first jet aircraft to go into regular passenger service. It began flying in 1952. It could fly fast enough to halve the travel time for many long journeys. By 1958 jet airplanes were common for travel between Britain and North America.

> Heliflight

In 1907 the French inventor Paul Cornu was the first person to design and build a powered aircraft that flew vertically. The first flight was very short. The machine lifted its inventor about 1 foot (.33 m) and the flight lasted about 20 seconds. The landing gear was made from four bicycle tires, which was very fitting as Cornu was a bicycle maker.

The Concorde

The droop-nosed Concorde supersonic passenger airliner flew from Britain and France to the USA for 27 years. The Concorde travelled at about twice the speed of sound and generally made the Atlantic crossing in 3½ hours—half the normal flight time. After a disastrous crash in Paris in 2000 the Concorde was eventually taken out of service.

Can You Believe It?

Parachutes

Parachutes were first designed in Europe in the fifteenth century. Leonardo da Vinci sketched a design during the period 1480–1483, but some historians believe that parachutes were used in China as early as the twelfth century. The first parachutes used silk as a material for the canopy and lines but modern designs use artificial fibers such as Dacron, Spectra, or Kevlar because they are lighter, stronger and do not stretch as much as silk.

Kites

The Chinese first made and used kites. In 400 BCE they used colorful kites in religious ceremonies and for military purposes. The kites were used to observe the enemy and for escaping from cities under siege. In recent years, kite flying has developed into a sport.

Amazing Paragliding Flight

In 2007 a German **paraglider**, Ewa Wisnierska, was caught in a storm in New South Wales, Australia and swept to an altitude of over 29,527 feet (9,000 m) —higher than the peak of Mount Everest. At about 19,685 feet (6,000 m), ice formed on Wisnierska's sunglasses before she blacked out because of lack of oxygen. After 40 minutes, she regained consciousness and flew her paraglider back to Earth, landing safely. When rescuers found her, she was still covered in ice.

Hang on

In 1922 George de Bothezat built a helicopter with four six-bladed **rotors**. It carried up to three passengers in more than 100 flights at McCook Field near Dayton, Ohio, USA. One of the passengers clung to the frame to show the machine's stability; however, the helicopter never rose higher than 16.4 feet (5 m).

Who Found Out?

Flight Design: Leonardo da Vinci

Leonardo da Vinci (1452–1519) was born near Florence in Italy. He was a great artist and inventor who designed and sketched many machines that were centuries ahead of their time. Among his machines were a tank, a submarine, a parachute, and a flying machine.

His flying machine was designed to be powered by a human passenger beating his arms like the wings of a bat. The design was based on Leonardo's careful study of the way the wings of birds and bats worked.

first flight:
Wilbur Wright and
Orville Wright

The Wright brothers, Wilbur (1867–1912) and Orville (1871–1948), are credited with being the first people to make a heavier-than-air controlled human flying machine. They experimented a great deal with gliders for a number of years, perfecting their propeller, engine, and steering designs.

On December 17, 1903, at Kitty Hawk, North Carolina, Orville flew their aircraft, the Wright Flyer, for 39 minutes at about 10 feet (3 m) off the ground. It was a very short and low flight but it was enough to encourage the brothers to develop their aircraft. They eventually built aircraft for the U.S. Army.

Daredevil Aviator:
Elizabeth (Bessie) Coleman

Bessie Coleman (1892–1926) was born in Waxahachie, Texas. When she was at the Colored Agricultural and Normal University in Langston, Oklahoma, she read about the Wright Brothers and Harriet Quimby, a woman pilot. She dreamed of becoming a pilot too, but at that time a black woman was not able to take flying lessons in the United States.

Bessie eventually learned to fly at the renowned Federation Aeronautique Internationale in France. She received her pilot's license in 1921, becoming the first American to obtain her license from the French aviation school and the first licensed black pilot in the United States.

In 1922, Bessie gave her first performance at an air show at Curtis Field, near New York City. Tragically, she died in an aircraft accident in Jacksonville, Florida, at the age of 34.

Kevlar:
Stephanie Kwolek

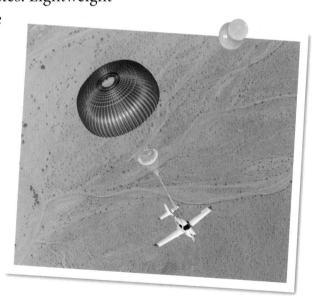

Stephanie Kwolek (1923–) is an American research scientist who invented the synthetic fiber Kevlar. Kevlar is five times stronger than steel and so is extremely strong for its weight. It is used a great deal in aviation, especially for safety helmets, aircraft panels, and parachutes. Lightweight materials such as Kevlar are very important in aviation, as things must be made as light as possible. Kevlar is also used to make light and effective bulletproof vests.

It's Quiz Time!

The pages where you can find the answers are shown in the red circles.

Unscramble these names of people connected with aviation

nemocal   ⑱

dazedethot   ⑮

kkeowl   ⑲

thgiwr   ⑰

Choose the correct words

1. (Helicopters, Bumblebees, Hovercraft) rotate their wings very quickly, at about (200, 20, 2000) beats a second. ⑧

2. The (Concrete, Concorde, Comet) supersonic passenger airliner flew from (Britain, Bahrain, Italy) and (Finland, France, Germany) to the USA for 27 years. ⑬

3. (The Hindenburg, The Harrier jump jet, The space shuttle) can land and take off (horizontally, vertically, at the speed of sound) like a (bumblebee, rocket, helicopter) but flies like a jet. ⑫

Complete these sentences

1. In 1922, George de Bothezat built a _____ with four six-bladed _____. ⑮

2. Kevlar was used as an aviation material because it is _____ and _____. It is also used to make _____ jackets. ⑭ & ⑲

3. The four forces that make flying possible are lift, thrust , _____ and _____. ④

4. _____ are the only engines powerful enough to overcome Earth's _____ and lift objects into _____. ⑪

Try It Out!

Do you remember reading about how flight works on page 4 and about gliders on page 7? We are going to make our own circle glider to see how flight works firsthand!

What You'll Need:
A straw, a 5-by-.5-inch (13 x 1 cm) strip of paper, a 7-by-1-inch (18 x 2.5 cm) strip of paper, tape.

What To Do:
Take the smaller strip of paper and make a circle with it. Tape it closed. Then take the longer strip and tape it into a circle. Now tape the circles onto either end of the straw. Throw it as you would a paper airplane, with the small circle toward the front. What happens?

Now Try This!

Try the same activity using different size strips of paper and straws of different lengths. What happens when you throw those gliders?

Glossary

airships (ER-ships) Any aircraft lighter than air containing hydrogen or helium.

boosters (BOO-sterz) Devices that increase power.

compressed (kum-PRESD) Flattened or squeezed by pressure.

denser (DENTS-er) Thicker; closely packed together.

dirigibles (DIR-uh-juh-belz) Types of airships with rigid structures, such as a zeppelin.

drag (DRAG) The force exerted by air surrounding a moving object that slows it down.

gravity (GRA-vih-tee) The force that pulls all the objects in the universe toward one another.

lift (LIFT) To force something upward, counteracting the force of gravity. Lift is produced by changing the speed and direction of a moving stream of air.

momentum (moh-MEN-tum) The amount of motion of a moving body.

orbiter (OR-buh-ter) A spacecraft designed to go into orbit; especially one not intended to land.

paraglider (PA-ruh-gly-der) A person who sits in a harness suspended below a fabric wing and launches himself or herself into the air from a great height.

propels (pruh-PELZ) Moves rapidly.

propellers (pruh-PEL-erz) Devices with blades that spin around to drive an aircraft (or ship).

rotors (ROH-terz) Parts of a machine that move in circles or rotate.

stability (stuh-BIH-luh-tee) Firmly fixed; not likely to be overturned.

thrust (THRUST) The propulsive force of a jet or rocket engine.

Index

Web Sites

Due to the changing nature of Internet links, PowerKids Press has developed an online list of Web sites related to the subject of this book. This site is updated regularly. Please use this link to access the list: *www.powerkidslinks.com/ssm/fly/*